AF571809

A Handful of Sand

Poems by

Robert H. Deluty

GATEWAY PRESS, INC.
Baltimore, MD 2007

Please direct all correspondence and book orders to:
Robert H. Deluty
4783 Ilkley Moor Lane
Ellicott City, Maryland 21043

Library of Congress Control Number 2007925668
ISBN-13 978-0-9792459-1-6

Published by
Gateway Press, Inc.
3600 Clipper Mill Rd., Suite 260
Baltimore, MD 21211-1953

Printed in the United States of America

To

Marvin, Evelyn,
Julie, and Alie

Other books by Robert H. Deluty
published by Gateway Press

Within and Between: Poems (2000)
The Long and Short of It: Essays and Poems (2003)
Observed and Imagined: Poems and Essays (2004)
The Essence of Moments: Poems (2004)
Treasuring the Details: Poems (2005)
Present Sense: New and Selected Poems (2005)
Glimpses and Snapshots: Poems (2005)
Specks and Flashes: Poems (2006)
Infinity in the Palm of One's Hand: Poems (2006)
Giving Subtilty to the Simple: Poems (2006)
In the Moment: Poems (2007)

Contents

8 philanthropist's child
a haiku poet
an out-of-towner
stares at the mirror
Judge Kowalski

9 asleep in his chair
renowned physicist
driving fifty-five
on a shooting star
an old mailman

10 a vegan checker
during her orals
maternity room
informing her child
a ninth grader

11 comedian's wake
a psychologist
rough neighborhood
two inches of snow
high school freshman

12 coffee break
after a good deed
his wife's birthday
death camp survivor
recycling day

13 grad student's mother
asking their rabbi
a kindergartner
a Muslim woman
at seventy-two

24 an acclaimed writer
Santa Fe resort
an obese woman
a cat-phobic man
mid-March

25 his grandmother
a tenement child
seated at Shea
their dachshund
in Abilene

26 Jewish football fans
a college freshman
her son's Christmas card
on the sidewalk
a teen with cancer

27 all-star linebacker
a balding man
five star restaurant
married twelve years (I)
married twelve years (II)

28 at *Hallmark*
a laughing child
Auburn's football coach
on a South Bronx bus
a shrink's waiting room

29 their great aunt
a demented man
dinner with the boss
a homeless couple
a baseball purist

30 singles bar
old ventriloquist
on the flight home
the eve of orals
post-miscarriage

31 her boyfriend's front porch
a ten-year-old boy
before the wedding
burping their baby
a safecracker

32 food for the soul
a hand surgeon
a Jewish husband
activists cancel
physician's office

33 inner city girls
choosing a coffin
a cheating husband
first-year med students
a carwash owner

34 obese man's widow
his Mom replying
during dinner
pre-honeymoon
a lost tourist

35 their son's funeral
a Japanese man
a wary mother
her new boyfriend
a girl in Bombay

36 his cell phone ringing
reading the obits
over brunch
a waiter's mother
frigid March morning

37 centenarian
a Jewish flutist
a shoplifter
during his address
her father-in-law

38 cruel, unusual
the committee chair
an author's mother
on television
his daughter's wedding

39 longtime professor
a five-year-old girl
an old collie
in Sunday School
a Manhattanite

41 *Quotation (Ralph Waldo Emerson)*

43 at the altar
disorganized crime
a friend's Doberman
a Yale professor
in Hawaii

44 a Jewish couple
telling her parents
a chirping rainbow
eight-year-old craftsman
a psychiatrist

61 trying to explain
household magic
an insomniac
mid-July
an Alabaman

62 a flower girl
opening a trunk
at commencement
mid-February
a panicking bride

63 in music class
a young novelist
exam eve
on the honeymoon
a six-year-old girl

64 2:40 a.m.
married two weeks
end-of-year review
their twelfth grader
pre dental visit

65 April sixteenth (I)
April sixteenth (II)
a job candidate
group therapy
Easter morning

66 an ill wind
a pink-haired teen
choosing not to tell
elderly teacher
an orphaned pig

67 underachiever
perfectionist
blithely referring
a weeping child
just before Christmas

68 world renowned scholar
high school reunion
trying to make clear
a rabbi's wife
1 p.m. class

69 Prague travel agent
driving past the cross
irate customer
after thirty years
young basketball fans

70 church choir's back row
an OCD man
on the expressway
a freshman queries
their son's date

71 on a crowded bus
an ill analyst
Greek/Chinese wedding
school librarian
choosing a toaster

72 Sabbath holy war
a pepper mill
Mrs. Washington
beside her boss
a Wall Street tycoon

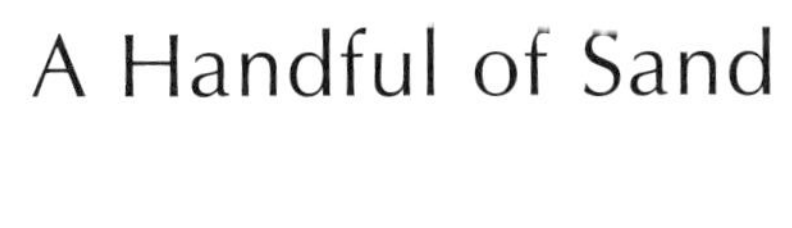

A Handful of Sand

A handful of sand is an anthology of the universe.

David McCord

clock repair shop …
a bipolar man staring
at a pendulum

therapist's mother
still bragging how early
he was toilet-trained

during the midterm
observing the proctor
playing solitaire

banquet tables …
his relatives are grouped
by their neuroses

in a hospice
quizzing her granddaughter
on state capitals

a weight-conscious girl
leaving skim milk and rice cakes
for Santa Claus

on the beach
a young patriot wearing
an Old Glory thong

a sixth grade teacher
asked whether Old Mexico
is also a state

smiling in his sleep …
a health food store owner
dreaming of *Fritos*

one day after
their youngest son moves out,
buying a white couch

Chinese adoptee
learning from her Jewish aunt
the meaning of *kvetch*

Little Italy …
eating his fourth pizza slice
while ogling his fifth

a Nobel chemist
preferring to be described
as a teacher

over dinner
a boy building a snowman
of mashed potatoes

living alone,
locking her bathroom door
before bathing

their first date ...
watching the waiter take back
her barely touched meal

on his deathbed
her grandfather belittling
a friend's get-well card

a twelve-year-old Jew
wonders if Jesus had fun
at *his* Bar Mitzvah

a newspaperman
unpacking a thesaurus
on his honeymoon

Christmas vacation ...
a boy spreads banana peels
on ice-covered steps

tattoo parlor ...
demanding a deep discount
for a misspelled spouse

a two-year-old
teaching his baby sister
how to high-five

turned down as best man,
his brother comes to the church
wearing pajamas

The Dark

A middle-aged historian
Choosing not to write
His own family's story
For fear of the dark:
The sad, the abnormal,
The evil and the unknown.

philanthropist's child ...
pleading for an increase
in her allowance

a haiku poet
thumbing through a garden guide
for stimulation

an out-of-towner
viewing a panhandler's plea
as a mugging

stares at the mirror
over her daughter's bed
hoping for the best

Judge Kowalski
overhearing a juror
tell a Polish joke

asleep in his chair
an old man's open mouth
entices a moth

renowned physicist
learning from his granddaughter
how to burn CDs

driving fifty-five
while eating fried chicken,
steering with his knees

on a shooting star
a three-year-old dog lover
wishing for paws

an old mailman
estimating all the shoes
he has worn out

a vegan checker
urging a young customer
to return the ham

during her orals
fighting a migraine fueled
by fear and caffeine

maternity room …
a sign on the door urging
Push, Push, Push

informing her child
the acorn stuck in his ear
will become an oak

a ninth grader
on a bus with poor shocks
applies eyeliner

comedian's wake …
his sons placing on each chair
a whoopee cushion

a psychologist
thanking her deranged parents
for inspiration

rough neighborhood …
a new driver is warned
never to honk

two inches of snow
closing all Maryland schools …
irate Maine students

high school freshman
hanging a car freshener
in his gym locker

coffee break …
a bank teller contemplates
the perfect crime

after a good deed
their child requesting money
rather than praise

his wife's birthday …
handing her a gift card
for a face-lift

death camp survivor
chides his grandson for whining
about no dessert

recycling day …
collecting from his neighbors
last week's magazines

grad student's mother
haranguing a professor
about her son's *B*

asking their rabbi
if he could work at *Macy's*
as a Santa Claus

a kindergartner
pets her sleeping dog, wonders
what is he dreaming

a Muslim woman
convinced that her heartburn
is pork-related

at seventy-two
first learning that, in high school,
he was deemed a stud

funeral parlor ...
a child screaming at a priest
to return her Dad

homeless man's Christmas ...
using a STOP sign and foil
to create a tree

driving a taxi
thinking about his twelve years
in private schools

a bored marksman
shooting the points off
a poinsettia

seeking to hurt Mom
he pleads with his fiancée
not to convert

final exam eve …
their procrastinating son
ironing his jeans

Christmas morning …
a schizophrenic woman
cursing agnostics

his college roommate
urging him to get stoned,
then watch *Fantasia*

anorexic teen
worried that the IV drip
will make her obese

first-year resident
asking a writhing patient
how's it going

a four-year-old girl
asking to borrow from Gramps
his prosthetic hook

ex-prostitute
inviting former clients
to her wedding

Lotto millionaire
driving home with his check,
fined for speeding

anger management …
a cab driver pocketing
a fifty-cent tip

atop a teen's head,
spiked orange hair appearing
radioactive

amateur fighter
entering the boxing ring
in a *Sears* bathrobe

poetry class ...
drawing on sitcom jingles
as his muse

in the men's room
asking his two-year-old
to keep her eyes shut

an old rabbi
dreams of being the victor
in a bar fight

on her birthday
a chemo patient shopping
for a Cher wig

a Southern Baptist
explains to her Sikh friend why
he's going to hell

depressed siblings
referring to their home
as *Prozac Acres*

April Fool's Day ...
a sleeping Dad has cat hair
taped to his bald head

pancake house ...
an alcoholic requests
a wine list

mid-life crisis ...
a house painter considers
portraiture

Perspective

It's been a hard life,
Said the old woman.
My parents treated me like dirt.
My brother is a crook.
My sister's psychotic.
My first husband left me
for a waitress.
My second, for an actor.
My son's been in and out
of prison and rehab.
But my daughter's the one
who broke my heart:
At thirty, she became a
Republican.

O young artist, you search for a subject—everything is a subject. Your subject is yourself, your impressions, your emotions in the presence of nature.

Eugène Delacroix

called a racist
for correcting a student
saying *ax* for *ask*

turnpike restroom …
the man in the next stall
roaring with laughter

a professor's child
explaining that he's too smart
for her college

at eighty-four
a Jew regrets burning off
her Auschwitz tattoo

Valentine's Day …
a young widow buys herself
heart-shaped chocolates

an acclaimed writer
using a Christmas fruitcake
as a paperweight

Santa Fe resort …
three Chinese businessmen
in ten-gallon hats

an obese woman
entertaining the grandkids
by wiggling her chins

a cat-phobic man
holding his daughter's kitten
at arm's length

mid-March ~ a cabbie
in a white, jeweled turban
and orange earmuffs

his grandmother
staring at the safety pin
in his girlfriend's ear

a tenement child
embarrassed to admit
he loves croquet

seated at Shea ...
seven consecutive fans,
six first languages

their dachshund
trying to chase a squirrel
up an oak tree

in Abilene
a young tourist inquiring
what *Tex* is short for

Jewish football fans
breaking their Shiva mourning
for bowl game updates

a college freshman
skipping a calculus quiz
to cheer up a friend

her son's Christmas card …
his signed first and last names
follow *Yours Truly*

on the sidewalk
their one-year-old grandchild
petting her shadow

a teen with cancer
pleading with his doctors
to be honest

all-star linebacker
at the bottom of a pile,
biting a finger

a balding man
looking at an old photo,
longs for his cowlick

five star restaurant …
warning her son not to drink
from the finger bowl

married twelve years,
turned on by a bead of sweat
on a coed's cheek

married twelve years,
repulsed by a bead of sweat
on his wife's cheek

at *Hallmark*
a mime selecting
a blank card

a laughing child
pointing at the ice cream scoop
on his sister's shoe

Auburn's football coach
stunned by the Ole Miss center
named Silverstein

on a South Bronx bus
a sixth grade student reading
Walt Whitman poems

a shrink's waiting room …
telling a gorgeous woman
he's not a patient

their great aunt
shouting at a slow busboy
she's too old to wait

a demented man
and his ten-year-old grandson
playing air guitars

dinner with the boss …
poking his wife in the ribs
to keep her awake

a homeless couple
sleeping in each other's arms
on a rush hour train

a baseball purist
chiding a girl for wearing
a pink Yankee cap

singles bar ...
his wedding ring falling through
a pants pocket hole

old ventriloquist
choosing a burial plot
for his partner

on the flight home
a halfback shows a punter
how to crochet

the eve of orals
a student grilling herself
while in a deep sleep

post-miscarriage ...
dreaming about a parade
of empty strollers

her boyfriend's front porch ~
an old, chipped toilet doubling
as a planter

a ten-year-old boy
using his new pogo stick
in the bathtub

before the wedding
the groom's mother checks his ears
for excess wax

burping their baby
as his wife tries to spoon-feed
her stroke-impaired Dad

a safecracker
exerting self-control
near a piggy bank

food for the soul …
a ribs joint standing beside
an A.M.E. church

a hand surgeon
choosing to buy insurance
from *Allstate*

a Jewish husband
shocked that his Gentile in-laws
don't use mayonnaise

activists cancel
a global-warming protest …
impending ice storm

physician's office …
waiting for the test results
with her pastor

inner city girls
walking past their street's signs …
Bail Bonds, Checks Cashed

choosing a coffin
from among Mom's shoeboxes
for his dead hamster

a cheating husband
writhing on a motel bed
as his wife gives birth

first-year med students
voting who among their peers
will be sued first

a carwash owner
smiles upon catching a glimpse
of a pigeon flock

obese man's widow
still sleeping on the left edge
of the bed they shared

his Mom replying
Okay upon being told
that he loves her

during dinner
regaling the grandchildren
with his bunion woes

pre-honeymoon ...
the groom's sisters urging him
not to be a schmuck

a lost tourist
spotting a car with the tag
SEEKGOD

their son's funeral ...
glared at by her husband
for sobbing loudly

a Japanese man
agape as he walks past
McCoy's Judo School

a wary mother
interviewing a sitter
named Lolita

her new boyfriend
shows off towels he's stolen
from four-star hotels

a girl in Bombay
terrified of an outbreak
of mad cow disease

his cell phone ringing
as he is pelted from behind
by movie popcorn

reading the obits …
weeping not for eight soldiers
but for a racehorse

over brunch
three bejeweled trophy wives
discussing prenups

a waiter's mother
bragging to her neighbors
how well he's tipped

frigid March morning …
a homeless child gives her doll
an extra blanket

centenarian
tying her wisps of white hair
in pigtails

a Jewish flutist
explains why she loves Wagner
to her incensed Dad

a shoplifter
making off with two copies
of a self-help book

during his address
the class valedictorian
fighting the giggles

her father-in-law
laughing to the brink of tears
at his own joke

cruel, unusual …
forcing their teenaged son
to read *Beowulf*

the committee chair
sucking a grape lollipop
during her orals

an author's mother
praying that his new book
is not a memoir

on television
a killer seeks forgiveness
from Oprah Winfrey

his daughter's wedding …
a poet scribbling feelings
on a tablecloth

longtime professor
viewing term paper grading
as doing penance

a five-year-old girl
placing on her basset hound
paper clip earrings

an old collie
sensing her master's sadness
before he does

in Sunday School
two fifth graders debating
the souls of gerbils

a Manhattanite
regarding all of Jersey
as semi-rural

A moment is a concentrated eternity.

Ralph Waldo Emerson

at the altar
the bride spotting the groom
checking his watch

disorganized crime …
each thief thinking the other
brought the tools

a friend's Doberman
perceiving his hand-raised *Hi*
as threatening

a Yale professor
asking his child's fiancé
to call him *Doctor*

in Hawaii
two tourists complaining
there's too much lava

a Jewish couple
naming their newborn twins
Connor and Seamus

telling her parents
she wants to be a psychic …
predicting their screams

a chirping rainbow …
six parakeets on a perch
in a pet store cage

eight-year-old craftsman
strings a Mother's Day necklace
of his baby teeth

a psychiatrist
shocking his long-term colleagues
by speaking of sin

a Greek immigrant
bragging about his grandson,
the genus

at the cleaners
removing from a trash bag
six Brooks Brothers suits

an old Chinese man
eating a red king crab leg
with jade chopsticks

the third sister
relishing her role
as the evil one

an English teacher
correcting the poor grammar
of his one-year-old

Friday the 13th ...
having a panic attack
in Disneyland

her six-year-old
requests a rake and shovel
to clean his room

ESL student
clearly enunciating
the *k* in *knowing*

For Elise and David

By deeds and by words
They would show and tell:
Be caring, be competent.
Do good and do well.

in church ~ a lady
and her gay adult son
in matching boas

Ice Capades …
playing *fetch* with his foxhound
on a frozen lake

gas station men's room …
the sounds from the next stall
suggesting childbirth

an older sister
convincing a three-year-old
that he was hatched

unprepared student
curses the falling snow
melting on contact

post-burial …
removing his Mom's number
from their speed dial

her cocker spaniel
failing to grasp the concept
of waxed fruit

darting in and out
of his neighbor's mailbox ~
a baby squirrel's tail

out of bandages
their son covers a knee scrape
with duct tape

her grandmother
screaming at a jaywalker
wearing earbuds

a boy pondering
the number of toothpicks
an oak tree would yield

on a dare
wearing a pink Gay Pride cap
in a redneck bar

a mid-winter drive …
grappling with street ice, sun glare
and a nauseous child

a desperate groom
asks his parole officer
to be his best man

third grade science class …
a girl asks where in the brain
love is stored

a married man
wondering why he's single
in all of his dreams

on a walk
their dog dragging a fir branch
four times her length

art supply store …
an inner-city painter
buying more gray

a snowstorm raging
as three housebound college boys
watch *Dude, Where's My Car?*

visiting scholar
teaching Yiddish idioms
at Notre Dame

Compromise

Sunday, 10:30 a.m. at
Dunkin' Donuts/Baskin Robbins.
A mother, a father, and
Their four-year-old son
Try to decide on breakfast.
The child demands a scoop
Of pistachio ice cream.
It's too early for that,
Says the mother.
The child counters with
A plea for an éclair.
That's no breakfast,
Asserts the father.
After five minutes of
Debate, tears, and tantrums,
The child gives in, accepting
A vanilla-frosted cruller.

at the free-throw line
a tense third-stringer praying
not to miss the rim

a child screaming
I never asked to be born …
Dad concedes the point

in an Irish bar
asserting that his surname
was once McLevy

warning her students
death is the only excuse
for arriving late

in his kitchen
an old mathematician
making pi puns

a contrite teen
re-plastering the crevasse
in the wall he punched

new Nazi defeat ...
death camp survivor teaching
his grandchild Hebrew

Christmas card photo ...
suspecting that her in-laws
have been airbrushed

learning from her son
that the friend sleeping over
is nicknamed *Pyro*

service station ...
using a squeegee/sponge
on his eyeglasses

college senior
misspelling *Randolph-Macon*
on her resumé

for show-and-tell
a kindergartner bringing
his new cell phone

barbershop quartet
struggling with a medley
of *ZZ Top* hits

an eight-year-old boy
cursing Grandpa for dying
on Christmas eve

his brother-in-law
treating a *No Smoking* sign
as a suggestion

ruminating why
his girlfriend chose a gay film
for their second date

her great-grandmother
dispensing weight-loss advice:
suck coat buttons

wearing high heels
a six-foot, two-inch woman
asks for a raise

eighty-year-old man
at his mother's funeral
cries he's an orphan

a Nobelist's den ...
his only framed diploma
is from high school

suicide hotline …
between calls, a counselor
taking *Zoloft*

unskilled at dunking,
a child scoops gingerbread
from a cup's bottom

post-surgery
asking for his appendix
as a memento

hearing a freshman
describe a renowned colleague
as *smart, but evil*

hearing a colleague
describe a clueless freshman
as *God's punishment*

sixtieth birthday …
a grandson presenting her
a *SpongeBob* lunchbox

in a plain casket
an old clown in a dark suit
and floppy shoes

replacing the face
of his third wife with his fourth
on the dartboard

AA meeting ends …
gum wrappers, cigarette butts
littering the floor

mid-nightmare …
an Orthodox rabbi
shucking oysters

But man must light for man
The fires no other can,
And find in his own eye
Where the strange crossroads lie.

David McCord

trying to explain
to a nine-year-old mourner
the need for death

household magic ...
watching twenties disappear
from his wallet

an insomniac
sitting in a board meeting,
daydreaming of sleep

mid-July ~ his son
grabbing an ice-filled cooler
and his snowboard

an Alabaman
denouncing Virginians
as Yankees

a flower girl
standing on her head
during the *I do's*

opening a trunk
belonging to his late Dad,
finding lace doilies

at commencement
a beach ball tossed from the stands
beaning the provost

mid-February …
Saudi tourists in Houston
fearing frostbite

a panicking bride
asking complete strangers
about pimple masks

in music class
a red-faced sophomore
mispronounces *fugue*

a young novelist
incensed with his editor
for the improvements

exam eve ~ holding
an oral thermometer
over a flame

on the honeymoon
learning that compromise
is not his strength

a six-year-old girl
requesting from her doctor
a cure for freckles

2:40 a.m. …
a cocaine addict's mother
staring at the phone

married two weeks …
editing his comments
about her meatloaf

end-of-year review …
an ugly-toed professor
urged to wear boots

their twelfth grader
choosing a four-year college
based on school mascot

pre dental visit …
realizing the dire need
to get an oil change

April sixteenth ...
three rookie accountants
swigging champagne

April sixteenth ...
a longtime C.P.A.
sleeping late

a job candidate
informed by an employee
the boss killed a man

group therapy ...
posing as a sex addict
to meet women

Easter morning ...
a chocoholic youngster
waking up at 5:00

an ill wind ~ holding
a smiley-face umbrella
turned inside-out

a pink-haired teen
complimenting a girlfriend
on her new Mohawk

choosing not to tell
the department chairman
his fly is open

elderly teacher
urging students to savor
each potato chip

an orphaned pig
drinking from the udder
of a kind cow

underachiever
showing off his report card …
only two D's

perfectionist
hiding her report card …
one B+

blithely referring
to her lecherous husband
as *frisky*

a weeping child
denied by her cruel Dad
a pet lion cub

just before Christmas
in English class, a boy learns
about clauses

world renowned scholar
demanding that his students
call him Tommy

high school reunion …
a hit man presents himself
as a broker

trying to make clear
to his irate three-year-old
why wants aren't needs

a rabbi's wife
combing scores of matzo flakes
from his chest-length beard

1 p.m. class …
their chemistry professor
reeks of alcohol

Prague travel agent
displaying picture postcards
from New Orleans

driving past the cross
constructed beside the road
where her grandson died

irate customer
assuming racial bias
instead of slowness

after thirty years
of publishing senryu,
trying a sonnet

young basketball fans
rooting for the college team
with the best tattoos

church choir's back row …
the pastor's tone-deaf child
lip-syncing the hymns

an OCD man
eating candy off the floor …
caramel trumps dirt

on the expressway …
spraying *Windex* with his left,
steering with his right

a freshman queries
whether New Mexicans
like Americans

their son's date …
UNLIMITED ACCESS
printed on her shirt

on a crowded bus
three middle school boys discuss
menstruation

an ill analyst
asking his patient to sit
while he lies down

Greek/Chinese wedding …
teaching his Shanghai in-laws
to dance like Zorba

school librarian
discovering hardcore porn
tucked in an atlas

choosing a toaster
as their wedding present
for two millionaires

Sabbath holy war …
New York Giant fans preaching
to the Jet faithful

a pepper mill
evokes from a child and dog
a shared sneeze

Mrs. Washington
informing a young bigot
she was born Sue Katz

beside her boss
muttering *What a douche bag*
a tad too loudly

a Wall Street tycoon
wanting to be remembered
for his kindness

on Yom Kippur
four friends rate their mothers
on guilt-induction

eyes half-closed,
mouth full of creamed corn …
her photo taken

over breakfast
searching for one undyed hair
on three daughters' heads

a gentleman
striving for chivalry,
deemed a chauvinist

garbage collector
daydreaming of someday
dressing up for work

a cartographer
refusing to stop and ask
for directions

after counseling,
a phobic patient fearing
only Asians

college chess team
demanding of their coach
one cheerleader

his fiancée
unwilling to bend down
to retrieve a dime

during math class
a teen computes the seconds
until retirement

suspicion mounts ...
their teenaged daughter seeking
a wrench and a mop

calling it quits ...
spotting canned asparagus
in her cupboard

watching his father
use a hacksaw to open
a child-proof bottle

after the divorce
having a heart tattooed
around an old scar

beside a well
a haiku poet wishing
not to dry up

Index of Poems' Original Sources

Some of the poems presented in this volume have been published or are "in press" elsewhere. Listed below are the titles of these poems and the journals in which they have appeared or soon will appear.

In **Modern Haiku:** *at* Hallmark

In **The Pegasus Review:** *a five-year-old girl; an author's mother; an English teacher; Compromise*

In **Timber Creek Review:** *a shoplifter; driving a taxi; final exam eve*

Author's Note

Dr. Robert H. Deluty is a psychology professor at the University of Maryland, Baltimore County. He was named UMBC's Presidential Teaching Professor in 2002 and is currently the Director of the Clinical Psychology Doctoral Program. He lives in Ellicott City, Maryland with his wife, Barbara, and their children, Laura and David. Dr. Deluty's poems have been published in *The Wall Street Journal, The Baltimore Sun, Welcome Home, Frogpond, Mediphors: A Literary Journal of the Health Professions,* and many other newspapers, journals, and anthologies. *A Handful of Sand* is his twelfth book.